Already the Flames

Already the Flames

Clive Watkins

WAYWISER

First published in 2014 by

THE WAYWISER PRESS

Bench House, 82 London Road, Chipping Norton, Oxon OX7 5FN, UK
P.O. Box 6205, Baltimore, MD 21206, USA
http://waywiser-press.com

Editor-in-Chief
Philip Hoy

Senior American Editor
Joseph Harrison

Associate Editors
Dora Malech   Eric McHenry   V. Penelope Pelizzon
Clive Watkins   Greg Williamson

Copyright © Clive Watkins, 2014

The right of Clive Watkins to be identified as the author of this work
has been asserted by him in accordance with the
Copyright, Designs and Patents Act of 1988.

All rights reserved

A CIP catalogue record for this book is available from the British Library

ISBN 978-1-904130-72-7

Printed and bound by
T.J. International Ltd., Padstow, Cornwall, PL28 8RW

Contents

I

The Escape	13
The House	14
The Stones	16
Stop Press	19
Children Running Beneath Trees	20
Surveillance	21
The Names	22
Manifesto	23
Conversation	24
The Cry	25
The President Flies Home	27

II

The Angel	31

III

Histories	41
Crime Story 1	42
Crime Story 2	44
Travel Story	46
Children's Story	49
Nursery Song	51
Rock-a-Bye	52

IV

Small Scenes from a Life	55

V

But Not Forgotten	63
Jane, Aged Twenty, Takes Tea at the Big House	64
Return	65
Peregrine	66
Welsh Pig	68
Five Wasps	69
Black Kites, Salty, Jesus Bird	71
The Hospital	72
Some Trees, Some Creatures	76
A Scattering of Ashes	78
How to Tell	80
Address Book	82
Tenure	83

VI

Pilgrim	87
Labourers in the Vineyard	90
The Wolf of Gubbio	91
Goshawk	92
Assisi	94
Madonna and Child	95
Paragliders	96

VII

The Rainbow	101

VIII

Nuit Blanche	113
Apple	114
A Pretty Position	115
At Middelburg	116
Ornithology at Sumburgh Head	117

Trumpets and Castanets	118
On the Coast of Phaeacia	120
Insignia	121
The Visit	122
The Cyclist	123
NOTES	125
ACKNOWLEDGEMENTS	129
A NOTE ABOUT THE AUTHOR	131

    On the threshold of day the proud voices
muttering unrepentant from the pit
    were a thin ripple of bird-song
and leaves flickering like tongues in the green light.

I

APOLLYON: By this I perceive thou art one of my subjects; for all that country is mine, and I am the Prince and god of it.

— John Bunyan

The Escape

after an etching by John McPake R.E.

The sleeper sleeping before the hearth
has escaped out of his own dream,
leaving behind
in these webbed greys and blues
half-hidden images of himself.

The fire is dense with blood,
a mute tongue.
Its brushed edges flutter
in that slot of iron and stone.
High under the tilted roof
the naked woman drifts.
Inscribed in her twin bodies,
her own palimpsest,
she bears in her flesh
the marks of his avid making.

At any moment
the colours may darken
and vanish to a point.

Outside, a track leads to the willows,
to the brown river,
to the place where soon the city,
with its warrens,
its permissive balconies of sunlight,
will be built.

The House

> A fence there was with gaps the eye
> could look clear through at earth and sky,
>
> until one night an architect
> turned up and, noting this effect,
>
> removed the spaces from the fence
> and from them built a residence.
>
> With nothing in between, how weird
> and foolish then the slats appeared.
>
> "Monstrous and vulgar!" cried the town;
> and so the council tore them down.
>
> The architect? Got clean away –
> to Afri- or Ameri-cay.
>
> – Christian Morgenstern, "Der Lattenzaun" ("The Paling Fence")

Seen from across the park in which it stands
the house shines as if with its own light –
flickerings within, flashings instantly subdued.

Or perhaps the imbricated sheets it is made from
are alive with the light that falls on them –
flakes of opalescent colour, bruise-green, sapphire.

Draw nearer and it is a house of windows,
slits of eyes that peer through into another place –
a town with tree-lined streets and houses of its own,

carts and trams, gardens set behind trim hedges,
bright and contained like the images in a child's history book;
and the men in their coats, the women in their long skirts,

walking there, are not after all reflections of ourselves
but entire lives lived in ignorance of us. On dull days,
or at night, its walls shimmer with their absence,

a polished dark we stand before and see our own faces
staring back. Pale and ghost-like, they vanish and appear
as the coruscations flare and fade, while from within

come rumblings, buffetings, the sounds of sudden collapse.
(Who knows if they look back at us? There are no doors:
no one has ever entered or come out.)

The architect who built this house absconded long ago.
He fashioned it from the dead space that ran
between the things of his world –

the gaps in a fence, the blank between gate and road,
between railway and church, a span of flooded trench.
There are those who want the thing demolished,

its trickery an affront. "Why must we tolerate," they demand,
"this fabrication set down in our midst,
its iridescent shingles, the scandalous deception of its panes?"

But it persists unasked-for, and so we turn away
to our own world of definite places, our well-lit meeting rooms,
our assemblies, our sonorous and timely deliberations.

The Stones

1

The yellow reading lamp clicks on,
darkness wincing into shadow:
a closed book-lined space –
desk, keyboard, telephone,
an empty cup.
Words must be found
that will lead out of this,
the dream of a common language
coming in the end to a single sound,
a gasp that touches nothing.

2

Spent paper, fictions of demonic guilt.

A banner the size of a house
affords the bearded face
its fixed vantage-point,
the air filled with obstructing smoke,
with furious howls of adoration.

A broken arm dangling at his side,
the others walking away between the houses.

3

Gross habit of genuflection,
fervid observance,
in a fragrance of haloed candles,
in a drift of incense,
to be snuffed –

mute self-importance
masked as legitimacy –
to be snuffed out.

4

Yielding in vivid ignorance
we mistrust
even our own blank disbelief,
its rational blinding
incandescence.

5

Meat sings on the hot wire.
Its smoky odours rise
between high courtyard walls
into the enclosed spaces of the evening –
iron, stone, the attenuated smell
of earth, of broken roses.
Time now to take their wine indoors,
to view the watercolours, the Russian sketches
his clean acids eat into the copper.

6

From concrete pits, barred lawns,
from spinneys meshed with wire,
the screams rise up, the wails, the shrieks,
the hiccuping roars, heavy animal farts,
slaverings, gnawing of split wood,
peeled sexual cries, clashing of teeth,
snorts, despairing coughs, spiked fetid sneers.

7

What are these engines,
these silent, iterative mouthings?
Shall we skip and caper
at the edge of the circle
or will the sharp whistlers whip us in?
The accusers will not be coy,
rolling the stones
over and over in their hands.
Dip oil, dip water, for wounds, for thirst.

Stop Press

When Aldo Ricci steps from the car,
linen jacket over one shoulder
slung, and strolls across the lawn –
cut sandstone, random juniper,

a style prodigal of space –
his pretty wife is giving Cook
her last instructions: the *civet de lièvre*
seasoned, the wine uncorked.

Along the street, white lilac flowers,
a soft disbursement, and his neighbour's
Porsche in the settling dusk shines.
The door yields to his key, and she with her

sweet-smelling airy embrace comes
to the hall to greet him – time yet
for a shower, for each to talk of the day;
takes his brief-case from him, his jacket,

and their earned evening has begun.
He leaves behind him boxed glass, papers,
the low hum of circuits each
with its fellows perfectly engaged.

It is this exact tolerance breeds
house and garden, his wife, their cook,
though he on the office-forecourt lies
ringed by police lights, the wrecked

Mercedes, its shrapnel spent, still blazing.
His hands, their pale palms upturned,
reach out beyond the plastic sheet.
The black cameras flash and whirr.

Children Running Beneath Trees

Their naked shoulders mottled with green shadow,
they scatter beneath the tall September trees
down lanes and byways silent for their passing.

Closed the shutters, closed the familiar doors;
on iron balconies only a light breeze stirring
and sticks that rattle in unwatered pots.

Where are they running to, these skinny children?
Their bare feet pattering on the hard dry earth
send up small clouds of white dust in their passing.

They run with arms outstretched, but no embrace
awaits them in these desolate yards and gardens,
for of those who would take them in not one remains.

They make no cry, though their eyes are full of anguish,
as they hurry on through the early evening light,
which slides across the walls where they are passing.

(Don't ask, my dear, what they are running from.)
And singly, now, in twos and threes, they vanish
through a fence, a doorway, behind the deserted school,

and, weight and substance lost, their blank hurry
is air, is empty motion, is nothingness,
as if some hurt had passed with their swift passing.

Then on the street the unremembering lamps,
fluttering moths, gleam of shuttered windows;
and in the rooms the stricken talk goes on.

September 2004

Surveillance

Sun glints off the car's black flank,
the rear-seat passenger armoured
behind one-way glass

in the jink and swerve of reflections:
crowded pavements,
government offices, shops,

an architecture of occupation and desire
through which he stares –
personage of glass,

of dazzling illegible light –
at shops, at offices,
at crowds on the pavement.

Overhead, the helicopter
maintains its pulse,
its traversing synoptic gaze.

The Names

Terrible things lie scattered on the street.
They must remain nameless, though the raw names
persist in the dark waiting to be found.

July 2005

Manifesto

The pamphlet wars were not yet over,
the election deferred two fields away

at the far end of a punishing weather
when they lay back at last

and thought of England, that draughty place
bowed under winter's furred occlusion.

Night-walkers troubled the streets,
and a lascivious eye winked across the tables –

frayed roses, bowls of lemon water.
Absolute power is a door into dreaming

(dangerous luminosity), but coercion, Sir,
implies free will – vanquished, to know

your tongue belongs now to another:
white shoulders cupped in cool hands,

pearls of light, bruised perishable things
of silk, of paper, manifestations

of impotence and desire and whatever
glozing fortune drops in your musky lap.

If addressed, you will reply with modesty and politeness.
If not addressed, you will not speak at all.

As if trembling on the brink of the next revelation,
the next politic blow, they stare at one another,

indignant dust, each hoping the other will do
what both desire but neither dares propose.

Conversation

Just out of sharp earshot two men are talking
as if in moonlight at the edge of a small wood –
not angry but earnest, some ancient quarrel recalled
that once would have led to knives and the shedding of blood.

Half-heard their far-off voices. On the shadowy landing
the woman listens for a moment, her pale eyes held
in the window's dark glass as she turns on the lamp,
knowing within her the terrible weight of the child.

The Cry

Startled out of sleep by a single cry –
dog-fox or owl – he rises from a dream
of empty rooms, of corridors, and waits,
    eyes open in the dark,

for the answering call from the cold garden – lust
or hunger or fear; but there is only the sound
of his own breath, of the wind's breath in the eaves,
    the dream whispering still

at the edge of his mind; and in the interval,
which may not be an interval at all,
he finds himself once more standing alone
    in a hall of shifting echoes –

faint words he cannot catch or, catching them,
cannot make sense of, as if unseen mouths,
muttering a dialect he almost knows,
    were about to speak his name;

and there a window opens in his dream –
dense snow like smoke-drift from a hidden fire
falling between the boughs of leafless trees
    that, clearing a moment, shows

the infinite mute muster of the stars;
and then across the waste come other sounds –
the insistent ring of steel beaten on steel,
    a shrill grinding of gears,

and, as if carried from a great way off,
a deeper surge of voices that might be singing –
joy or lamentation he cannot say;
    and in his dream he turns,

the window gone, and dreams himself awake:
rank upon serried rank, the trees stand round,
tunnels of rustling shadow and the cry
    caught in his own throat.

The President Flies Home

The choir of bees forsakes the garden
    etcetera etcetera.
Grain rots in the storehouse.
The President flies home from Nice.
    Places, honours, preferments,
    titles, countries, kingdoms …
The bees forsake the garden.

The cypress is a shaft of sable flame
    etcetera etcetera.
The sharpest elbows reach the front.
To bring peace he slaughters half the country.
    … titles, countries, kingdoms,
    lusts, pleasures, delights …
The cypress is a shaft of flame.

A green halo gathers round the sun
    etcetera etcetera.
The headsman kills another hostage.
She puts her coffee down and signs the warrant.
    … lusts, pleasures, delights,
    bawds, wives, husbands, children …
A halo gathers round the sun.

Bells jangle in the white tower
    etcetera etcetera.
They flay his face and post it to the widow.
The villages are burned for sport.
    … bawds, wives, husbands, children,
    masters, servants, bodies, blood …
Bells jangle in the tower.

A small dog barks furiously at nothing
    etcetera etcetera.
The raped girl survives two days.
Politician and millionaire take cocktails on deck.
    … *masters, servants, bodies, blood,*
    juggling, cheats, fools, knaves …
A small dog barks at nothing.

Bee. Cypress. Sun. Bell. Dog.
    Etcetera etcetera.
    Etcetera etcetera.

II

The Angel

Let every soule submyt him selfe unto the authorytye of the hygher powers for there is no power but of God. The powers that be are ordeyned of God, but they that resest or are agaynste the ordinaunce of God shall receyve to them selves utter damnacion.

> – *Romans*, 13:1-2, unknown translator: inscription c.1550,
> St Peter's, Wenhaston, Suffolk

1

Wheeling above the river and its wharves,
above towers of sky-reflecting glass –
bronze, steel-blue, ice-blue – she flies,

still wary, still not losing height, her subtle ears
catching from the city's far-off shafts and trenches
where soon she must descend its thin abstracted roar –

unceasing pour of words, dull undertone of traffic,
hum of wires, all choiring together in the wind
that whips and burns off the sea …

2

John Bunyan would have had none of this.
Though Faithful's adversaries scourged and buffeted him,
cut his flesh with knives, stoned him and – last cruelty –

burnt him to ashes at the stake, salvation was at hand.
Unseen by the crowd, a chariot awaited,
as shown in my pocket-size Victorian copy,

its apple-green cover bruised, its pages foxed,
which was my father's once:
a confident print no bigger than my thumb,

in which the soul whirrs heavenwards on a cloud,
furnished with miniature martyr's crown
and two attendant angels, while far below

the body, reduced by distance, chained at the waist,
its hands composed in prayer, comes to a glorious end.
In Eunice Bagster's wiry image, those watching

are ghost-figures, their waving arms white stumps,
their heads mere blobs, the printer's darks reserved
for chariot, angels, soul and burning man.

What, I wonder, would she have made
of Nicholas Peke, arraigned and burnt in 1538,
denying to the last,

though scorched as black as soot and spitting blood,
his persecutors' ruthless faith,
or those who at the Bishop's proclamation –

forty days' indulgence
for all who fetched a stick to the heretic's burning –
rose from their seats and with their swords

cut branches down and cast them on the fire?
In Foxe's woodcut – dense, austere –
the tongues of flame coil round the heaped faggots:

enacted image of the Last Day,
tormented flesh witnessing against itself
to the frail materiality of spirit.

3

Stuck by the bronze spear between collar-bone and neck,
his foe's exact thrust,
he was borne down in a wave of anger and hate

and pinned fast to the earth;
yet still Achilles' grip on the ash-shaft
did not relent though its length encumbered him.

Zeus's golden beam had dipped. At the twin fountains,
one hot, one icy cold, by the stone troughs
where once the Trojan women had washed the clothes,

Athena tricked great Hector into combat.
Knowing itself deceived, his soul took flight,
wailing, to the sullen halls of the dead.

The gods looked on. They saw how it would end –
Achilles slain, Troy plundered and in flames,
the perilous voyages, home or into exile.

Stripped of its armour, his body lay in the dust,
and at last the warriors Achilles had held back
crowded round, admiring Hector's beauty and strength,

mocking him dead, and not one but left on him a wound,
their bare arms rising and falling, their blades flashing,
as through him they jabbed and hacked.

4

On the ceiling of Santa Maria del Fiore
the saved observe from their tiered seats –
as we from the marble pavement far below –

the damned descending into hell, their bodies flailing,
herded by winged demons down
to the inexorable fire and their allotted pain.

They float as if weightless in that vast space,
theatrical and enclosed. Yet climb up the dull tunnel
inside the dome to view them from the balcony,

and they are gross and carnal, the dizzying prospect
mere scene-painting, a clever trick
wrought by scale and distance on belief.

*

In Wenhaston's mediaeval Doom –
painted on oak boards and mounted, once,
above the chancel arch – the risen dead are naked.

Their limbs are slim and pale,
and equally tender, it seems, to pain or joy.
Those on Christ's right hand ascend

the stone stair to heaven, where they are received
by a gently smiling angel in a red robe
while, on his left, the damned are bound in chains

and led down by a team of grimacing devils
to the fanged mouth of hell.
No need to show their torments. Who did not know

the modes of such judicial savagery?
These little scenes encompass a whole world,
from heaven's castle keep,

buttressed in space, geometrical and firm,
to a hell that falls in curves to formlessness.
How did such things survive?

Concealed in barns, buried under middens,
sold as timber and given back again,
or, as here, distempered and replaced

by the royal arms and a monitory text –
to wait unseen three centuries or more
till workmen, not knowing what they had,

dismantled it and stacked it overnight
in the graveyard to make a bonfire of,
where a summer downpour washed the panels clear.

*

January, early morning, the air sharp with cold:
St Martin's, *Tumes-tun* – Thompson, in Norfolk –
stripped and cleansed by the fierce iconoclasms

though spared the restorer's zealous art.
Hoar-frost spangles every leafless bough
and the rough grass around the graves.

Is light itself the only element? The sun
strikes through chancel and nave,
across plain walls, unvarnished benches

and the delicate screen stencilled with pale flowers,
kindling in wood and stone a powdery gleam
as if to make a virtue of erasure.

5

Who would give countenance to those
who ordered out by families
the men and women and children into the square

and forced them down
to grub with their bare hands
the grass and weeds from between the stones;

then marched them to a barn and shut them in,
and, pouring on fuel, set the barn alight,
so that at least three hundred died?

Their screams ascended with the smoke and flames.
Who would give countenance to such,
or sit with those who offered to excuse them?

6

Bunyan, the Bible, your Book of Common Prayer,
talismans of a salvation you believed in –
on every voyage these went with you,

stowed in your officer's green-cloth case
among shirts and underwear.
Inside the cover of your *Pilgrim's Progress*,

a gift for your eighth birthday given
in the year an earlier war had ended,
your grandfather inscribed a dedication,

his hand unformed, the ink long turned to brown –
a blessing for a journey.
When the sky broke into fire

and all across Europe cities burned,
when the narrow seas were choked with ice
and spray stung and froze,

when, in the Scarpanto Strait,
a bomb ripped open the quarterdeck,
and *Sirius* – "Heaven's light our guide" –

limped off to safety with her many dead,
what angel did you think watched over you,
born with the caul close about your head,

fabled preservative against drowning,
which your mother till the day she died
kept in an envelope in her Bible?

Coming three times to Malta,
once under heavy attack –
men struggling in the water,

the water ablaze,
and you obliged to look on helplessly –
you thought of Paul and how your courses crossed.

In Athens, for instance, upon Mars Hill,
where he had declared the Athenian religion
a species of false consciousness

which Christ would judge on the appointed day.
Storm-tossed, no sign of sun or moon and all hope gone,
he came under guard from Crete,

but an angel appeared beside him in the night
to say: Be of good cheer, fear not,
for you must stand before the Emperor.

Destined for martyrdom, he would sail on,
Castor and Pollux clear in the night sky,
while you, who did not drown, sailed home.

Where two seas met, his ship was driven ashore,
and all were saved as it had been foretold;
and when a viper hidden in the sticks

fastened upon his hand, he felt no harm
but shook the thing off into the fire.
It hissed and writhed and bubbled and was consumed.

7

… Hesitant still, she descends a little,
knowing it is not salvation she will bring
to these glittering citadels,

*but hail and fire mingled with blood,
a star crashing to earth, a great wind
and the dead lying in the streets.*

III

Upanddown
Upanddown
rides the Almighty
in the elevator
of all elevators
on rainy weekends

– Alfred Brendel

Histories

In this story, you were the messenger whose message was believed in time: the wicked city would survive for one more year. In that story, you stood in the shadow of high rocks and parted from your brother.

In this story, you were set adrift on a reedy river to escape into someone else's myth. In that story, you were one of those whose names were turned to stone: black, indecipherable mirror.

In this story, the rings, the stunning necklaces and collars that you wore revealed in what rapture they had found you. In that story, the curtains winced, and your eyes looked out on blackness: a possible snow, a possible star.

In this story, the future went on unfolding like a conjurer's hat. In that story, you were the one who dreamed yourself into a hole and had to shut the door behind for fear the angel found you there.

Crime Story 1

Not, surely, the Gardener's Boy
dragged into the Study just like that
to stand cap in hand on the rug,
this grubby tousle-haired diabolus ex machina
of whom till this very moment we have heard nothing?
He brings with him from the compost he has been turning
a scent of sweet decay,
his knuckles bloodied where he caught them, he says,
on the rough timber of the bin.
Of whom we have heard nothing.
And yet three days before Christmas he must –
for so we are asked to believe –
have found his way unnoticed into the Kitchen
and poisoned with belladonna the warm posset
Cook had prepared for the Colonel's bed-ridden Aunt.
And only last week, concealed in a deep embrasure
behind the Library's floor-length curtains,
he thrust with his Grandfather's knife
at the lean young Curate
and mortally wounded instead
the Daughter of the House
(whom he had got with child)
before slipping unseen out of the window
and off through the rustling laurels.
Now at last the House Guests' baffled terror
may be allayed – as indeed it is,
everyone persuaded in an instant
that the Great Detective is entirely right.
This malevolent imp it was
brought all this wickedness to pass:
the woman lying dead upstairs,
the girl deflowered,
the shocking blood spilled on the pale carpet.
All along it was him and no one else.
And with this sly belated revelation

our Author bids farewell,
bequeathing in the pages of his book
a token of an order of a kind –
which we may ponder if we will
in the moments that remain
before the lights go out, our limbs relax
and patiently we address ourselves to the dark.

Crime Story 2

Clown Face running out of the bank,
pistol in hand, a hold-all tucked under one arm,
at his heels Ronald Reagan with a sawn-off shotgun,
the teller bleeding on the floor.
Or Stocking Head running from the jeweller's,
machete in hand, a black satchel under one arm,
the jeweller's assistant bleeding on the floor.
A young woman bleeding on the street.
Or Clown Face and Stocking Head
breaking into the gallery,
jumping into a get-away car – Audi/Ford/Škoda,
burning rubber vanishing up the street.

An inside job: someone shut off the alarm,
disconnected the panic button.
The gallery owner is sleeping with the politician,
the bank manager's wife is sleeping alone.
Ronald Reagan is an American President.

A Škoda ablaze on waste ground near the river,
ditto a Ford behind the derelict bakery,
elsewhere a grey Audi ditto ditto.
The teller dying later that day in hospital.
Or surviving long enough to help the police
and then dying. The young woman dying.

Studying the camera footage,
the inspector and her sergeant,
days and days and days: time to go,
someone is running out of time,
time out of mind, is doing time,
was not there at the time, timed to perfection.
And the inspector knowing all about it –
that is, the manager's wife and the politician –
but keeping shtumm:

the politician is her sister,
or the politician is not her sister but her brother,
or her brother is a politician.

Somewhere else a Škoda.
Stocking Head is not a cardiologist.
The inspector is not a woman.
Ronald Reagan is not an American President.
Clown Face is not Charlie Cairoli.

Travel Story

1

Though Federico Buonvincitore,
Chairman of Panglobal Securities Incorporated,
has crossed the Atlantic in his Learjet
countless times
and owns apartments
in Zürich, Paris, Rome, New York,
he hates flying,
he hates travelling.
The slightest swell makes him sick.
For this reason he confines his journeys
to those dictated
by calls of business alone.
In the grounds of his Cotswolds mansion
he has had built
from timber, stone, steel, sheets of moulded resin
a relief map of the earth,
a scale-model covering a quarter of an acre
complete with seas and rivers and mountains.
A fifteen-minute stroll encompasses
the whole world.
From almost any standpoint
he can survey
its great cities –
Panglobal has interests in them all.
When he dies aged fifty-eight
his young widow
in a private ceremony
scatters his ashes
across all seven continents
before flying off to an unknown destination.
The finer particles
that once were Federico,
caught up on the breeze,

go swirling northwards
across the Gobi Desert, across Siberia
and, drifting at last out over the ornamental lake –
c.1750, Lancelot "Capability" Brown –
slip, white dust into black water,
modestly from view.

2

When the ghost of Federico Buonvincitore
comes to the river
he expects
serpents like scaly shadows,
the seethe of tiny fish,
but there is only
the current's untroubled force.
Much to his surprise
he steps out
and walks lightly to the other bank.
      But where are the monopods, he thinks,
      the anthropophagi?
When the ghost of Federico Buonvincitore
comes to the desert
he expects
stone, sand, a basilisk sun,
torments of thirst.
He suffers none of these afflictions, however,
but passes easily over
seeing everything,
hearing, smelling, touching, tasting
nothing.
      And the phoenix?
When the ghost of Federico Buonvincitore
comes to the mountains
he expects dragons, ogres, trolls
but need not have feared.
Bodiless, weightless,
he rises over the highest peaks,

floats across the most fearful of chasms
and comes lightly down into a land of ice.
        The unicorn? The manticore?
And so his ghost continues
knowing now it will never reach
the end of the world,
a wisp of longing
still undetained
by any casual miracle it meets.

Children's Story

When at first light he crawls
from his cave, his den, his lair
or wherever it is he lives
and goes lolloping off
on two legs through the trees
who sees him?
        Lolloping? Cave?
        But who sees him?
The fire of his eyes,
the shambles of his breath,
his hooked shadow accompanying him.
When he comes to the village
everyone has already run away.
What will he do?
What will he do next?
Will he smash down the fences in a rage?
Will he shit on the rows of cabbages and beans?
Will he squeal and roar and fall asleep in the shade?
He yawns and yawns,
then sits his enormous rump on a large rock
and slowly begins
        slowly slowly
to gnaw at his own flesh
devouring
first one foot, then the other,
then a leg, and a leg,
one arm and the other.
His teeth gape so wide his neck strains
and the terrible shaft of his head
is one huge mouth,
his gullet a pulsing muscle of darkness
into which
with a crunch, with a suck, with a gulp
he entirely disappears
leaving behind on the sunshiny air

nothing but a round black stain,
a blind spot in the day,
and the only sound
is a faint bubbling eructation
>	once
>	no
>	twice.

Then the black stain
is a black stone lying in the grass
which a boy emerging from the forest
picks up for its deep opacity.
He will pierce it and thread it on a thong
for his girl to wear at her white throat.

Nursery Song

And the Little One said
Roll over, roll over,
and they did, they did.

The moon sang its chalky hymn
above the graves,
the yew trees spread
their cloak of shade,
and one fell out and one fell out
but nobody missed them where they fell,
a bone, a bone and yet another
higgledy-piggledy
into the earth.

And more arrived and more and more –
roll over, roll over –
and the Little One said Ah,
said Ah, said
One day they will let me sleep
my long sleep alone.

Rock-a-Bye

The tree sways,
>rock-a-bye
baby, and here we go
>tumbling
out of the snug nest
>all the way
down down
>into the dark.
Fathoms below,
>the talking
stones,
>the nameless faces
upturned.
>We stretch out
our arms a little as if
>to fly but just
keep on
>falling.

IV

Small Scenes from a Life

for T.B. (1937 – 2001)

… je me suis gardé léger
pour que la barque enfonce moins.

– Philippe Jaccottet

Sunlit Fields

In the cold morning air, running, you run.
Not tired yet, no need to turn for home,
no need to think how far your legs have brought you –
out of the garden, down through the silent wood,
across the stream and into the sunlit fields.
No need for thought at all. Lightly you tread:
your long stride will bring you safely back.

Shower, Breakfast

Dripping from knees and chin, you stand on the mat,
stark naked, a towel in your hand, and wait.
A pause, a flicker of time, and your ghost-self –
bowed head, thin shoulders, the grey hair of your groin –
steps calmly from the shower after you.
Later, in the kitchen, that dazzling space
that yawns from door to window, you wait again,
perfectly still, the statue of yourself,
while it catches up once more. You sit. You eat.

Waterfowl

In long unravelling lines, in ragged vees,
the waterfowl have returned to the salt-marsh.
Their calls carry across the shining pool

and up the hill to where, on this bright morning,
you sit at your desk and, hearing their distant cries,
open your notebook and uncap your pen.
Its gold nib poised above the unwritten page,
you close your eyes and listen; and so it begins.

Jigsaw

And so it begins: the slurs and slippages,
the lacework of misremembering and forgetting,
the word at the tip of your tongue you cannot speak,
the name, the place, the date, it rhymes with tree,
it rhymes with house, with stone, a gap to fill
like the gap in a jigsaw puzzle that needs a piece
of a certain shape, of a certain colour and line,
to make the broken image disclose itself,
for which even now your slow fingers search
in the scatter of pieces on the dining-table,
matching each to the one she puts in your hand.

Attic

For this you can find no words. Last learned, first lost,
already English betrays you, frays and thins
in quirky shreds and incoherences,
things read, things half-remembered which you patch
with the elegant French of your post-war Paris days.
You know how it will end. The French will fade,
and the German that you picked up in the camps,
till all that remains are a few stray scraps of speech,
a boy's unfinished Czech, a boy of five
concealed with his small sister in the attic.
Snow eases under the eaves. They shiver and wait,
hugging themselves to silence in the cold.

Private Library

Somewhere in all these books you know you will find
the thing you have been searching for for days:
mother father house tree stone.
You take them down from the shelves one by one,
turning their blank pages back and forth.
Hundreds of books remain for you to check.

Winter Night

From the porch door you look out at the night:
the sky salted with stars, the frozen fields
glimmering across the vale. No time, no time.
And you were not permitted even once
to put your arms around his neck before
the whirlwind swept him for ever into the dark –
who knew in that instant both of you were shades.

Box of Letters

You want them all destroyed, thrown on the fire
with the dead leaves the gardener has raked
in heaps against the wall, bundles of paper
bound with faded ribbon, inscribed from edge
to edge in spiky, once-familiar hands –
feathery airmail, scraps of coarser stuff
dispatched from places that have changed their names
or now no longer exist. You loosen one,
and at your touch it flakes into separate sheets,
line after line of sundered conversation,
and you perhaps the only one who remembers.
It's too late now. Let's put them back, she says.
The gardener has lit his fire already,
already the flames have crackled and leapt up
in a column of blue smoke, and a plume of ash

drifts as if weightless into the empty copse.
You watch from your window, hear in the next room
the muffled voices talking still of you.

Home

Caught between rage and terror, desolate,
you weep for her to take you home again,
but she sits on in your window seat and waits,
a silhouette, her frail hands in her lap,
till you come back once more from that far place
where, from first light to dusk, in sun, in wind,
on the cold step, a blanket round her head,
the woman sat and scanned the ruined square
from which the lorries days ago departed.

Rainy Afternoon

All afternoon it has rained; all afternoon
you sit in your arm-chair, lips and hands unmoving,
a stillness that is not a kind of sleep.
A watery light falls on your books, your desk,
your photographs, on the white round of your cup,
on the small stones you brought back from your walks –
smoke-grey, goose-grey, jet – and laid in a line
along the hearth. Rain patters at the window;
and your little terracotta hearth-goddess
stands into shadow as if into her own absence.

Day Out

The tide has turned. Flooding in little runs
up the deep gullies, it drives the screaming gulls
and oyster-catchers ahead of it over the flats
and stirs the tilted boats, their tackle clinking.
An onshore breeze riffles the stiff cord grass.

Beyond is the Thames you can no longer name,
a strip of milky green, and the nameless chimneys
on the far shore. The muddy channels fill;
the boats float off; the feeding grounds are gone.
A girl in a red jersey pulls for the moorings.
Now tiny white-caps break on the stone revetment.
You tug at your woollen scarf. And this is all.

V

Hector: We have been too long here. We do not live in this house: we haunt it.

– G. B. Shaw

But Not Forgotten

It is dark in this place. How long have I been here? Months? Years? The darkness has a settled feel. It is hard to disturb. Sounds reach me from the house. Feet tap along the hall, clump on the stairs somewhere above my head. Scratscratscrat: mouse-noise. Cat-noise is silence. The house eases into age. Once, I walked the rooms of this house. Once, I walked in other places. I have forgotten the rooms. I have forgotten the passageways their lives move through. I have been here a long time. They think they have forgotten me, but it's not true. They put me in this place, after all, made sure I was comfortable. At first they gave me food and good things to drink. Now I eat dust, I eat darkness. At first they left open the narrow door. The smell of their lives still reached me. Then the door closed. It was a long time before they remembered. I think they were surprised to find me still here. They are afraid of me. Sometimes I catch their voices from far off. They talk as if I had gone away. I answer. I do not think they hear my reply. My words are like dead leaves which eddy without meaning in their lives. I am shrinking, I am dwindling to a stubborn grain of darkness. I am becoming like the dust I eat. They are so self-possessed they think I have gone at last. But I shall stick. Like earth. Like air. Like the slow gestures, the sloughed words they have inherited from me.

Jane, Aged Twenty, Takes Tea at the Big House

Ting tang goes the jewelled clock, and the little painted
lovers bow and turn with graceful passion
on their gilded floor as if, so long acquainted,
they thought their intricate postures still in fashion.
Beyond, an oriel shows the garden: rolling
lawns, neat shrubs where a sly satyr gazes
hunched in the leaves, his stony eye controlling
from lake to quincunx that wide vista – mazes
of shadow piercing a wilderness created
for delight. But, without more ado, *Ting
ting* insists Aunt's bell, though, undefeated,
Jane taps her crop against her boot as if nothing
in all that world could prick her natural pleasure
in coming to tea, who is her Aunt's best treasure.

Return

Down-valley, the pastoral farms, the small town –
craft-shop, whole-food restaurant, museum:
protected under glass, political tracts,
impenetrable Welsh Bibles, brown-flecked prints;
shawls, flannels; the gear of antique trades;
in its plain wooden case, the stuffed skin
of the freak two-headed lamb ("born 1890,
survived ten days"), its wool a livid rust.

Up-valley, lake and dam, the mountain's hewn
cloud, vernacular grit that remains itself,
rinsing out of the leaden heaps as if
rain had turned to stone; a single phone-box,
a single house, clothes heavy on the line.
In that dense, greenish light, where else to go?

Dylife, Powys

Peregrine

Book

The book is a black stone, a stone box his father opens.
The hinge creaks. On the altar of the kitchen table,
beneath the earthenware jars on their high shelf,
between the scullery and the cast-iron range,
the washing in its basket, the scoured board,
the box lies open, the black book of stone.
His father reads from it through the bush of his beard:
*He placed at the east of the garden of Eden
Cherubims, and a flaming sword.*
The stink of the black words lifts off the page,
hangs like smoke beneath the rafters.
His mother's bright wings are folded.

White Mare

Out on the hill, the wind that blows round the world
rocks his boy's body: its cold hands
press against him as they pass.
Bird-like, he leans into its lift and swerve.
When he comes down from the mountain,
the white mare grazing in the field shies,
rippling the smooth muscles of her flank.
He wants to ride her, but she gallops off
into the shadow of the ash trees.

Egg

Softly he lifts the veneered casket from the shelf above his desk,
with a flick of his thumb snicks the brass catch back,
tilts up the lid: *Falco peregrinus*,
whose hooked vertical drop will burst its victim's skull.

Hedge, wall, gate: through the window, a rainy sun.

In its nest of wool, the single rust-brown egg glows with emptiness,
with the smoky marmoreal translucence of its death.
Its fecund substance blurted into the air, the hole it was blown through
is stopped with wax and turned away from the light.

Welsh Pig

Stiff-backed, trousered in his own ochreous muck,
he trots on tip-toe daintily towards me
as I open the wire-and-timber gate of his sanctum.
He grunts in the resonant note of his tight body –
not a greeting, not a challenge, either – and stops,
his trotters in possession of the earth,
a pig's length away. My flesh furrows his snout,
and I think of the teeth in his hooked and bristling jaw,
the ripe tomb of his den: straw-shine, shit-shine.
But he is at home here: I am no threat to him.
Crossing my path, he clips down the waste slate
to root among willow and birch beside the stream.
I observe the sprung wire of his tail, his trim
buttocks, the neat tucked peach of his balls.

Five Wasps

for Bob Etherington (1931 – 2013)

On the white sill of my little hotel room
three wasps lie dead, their black and yellow bodies
cramped and curled like tiny bristling hooks,
still venomous in death. Drawn to the light,
they butted out their lives on the cold pane.
Beyond the window the late-September sun,
watery and mild, breaks across the fell,
a sharp wind buffets the wood, the beck is roaring –
and now here's a fourth, a live one, buzzing up
from the apple core I left on the wash-stand.
It flies into the window's deep embrasure
where I crush it with a map against the glass.
So, how are they getting in? I ask the girl
who draws my evening pint in the residents' snug.
A nest in the wall, she says, *beneath the sill*;
and I imagine the frail papery cell
lodged in the dark between the canted slates –
their laborious hum, their long homing flights
for the last late-fallen fruit, last insect prey,
last gobbets of sweet carrion, before the cold
returns to crisp them in their banded shell.
And overnight indeed the weather clears –
frost on the scarlet hips in the little garden,
frost on the bracken and scrub along the fell,
a fringe of ice where the beck goes jouncing down
through the sunless gill over rocks the colour of blood.
My final day: I climb the ancient track
to the small tarn and the broad summit ridge.
The wind, shrill harbinger of fiercer cold,
flies howling upon me as if it would bear off
the one unrooted thing in this stony place.
On the far slope cloud-shadows stream away
past intake, fold and garth, while wave upon wave
beyond the crags that close the valley in

the higher fells unroll. They glitter as if
with snow-light in the bright, abounding air.
But now this evening, crossing from the shower,
my bare foot finds a fifth – dead, though its sting
pierces my heel with a needle of quick pain.
The kindled smart cools to a fiery ache,
but I am weary from my walk and know
sleep will come soon. – A last look at the sky:
the moon is up, and fine stars prick out
the roof of heaven in zones of wintry jet.
I dream and am the tenant of my dream:
stone, and grass, and the tarn as hard as iron,
and this pattering in the round cave of my skull –
the wind's dry ghost, the white whisper of frost
fastening itself once more on berry and leaf,
the rustle of wings housed in the frozen rock.

Great Langdale

Black Kites, Salty, Jesus Bird

Shafts of speargrass, pandanus and the high banks of the Dry
confine our gaze to slack brown water, red lilies
and glimpses through clumps of paper-bark and scrub
to the ochre cliffs of the Arnhem Land plateau.
The boat idles and slows. We lift our heads,
scanning the mid-day glare for the kites –
dots, motes in the dazzled eye,
flakes of ash caught in the earth's hot updraft,
wheeling and wheeling over floodplain and fissured scarp.
Now at the swing of the boatman's arm,
the upward arc of the bait out over the water,
here they come dropping with folded wings
from the fiery zenith,
black sun-stones, plummeting black stars.
Close over our heads they plunge and rise,
a quarrel of feathers and air, of beak and claw.
Cameras' repeated staccato, triggering of blurred images,
seconds of captured video – juddery, dislocated;
then the spacious upward sweep, the steep recession
into watchful invisibility.
Beneath the bank, still as a log in the sluggish water,
the salty hangs, and the Jesus bird he will never catch
stalks away into its own life across quaking lily-pads.

Yellow River, Northern Territory, Australia

The Hospital

Liverpool, 1950s

Deep Cutting

From a black hole in the earth out it comes roaring
a quarter of a mile through the deep sunless trench,

a live thing veiled in flame and livid smoke.
Two boys, their eager faces smudged with soot,

lean from the bridge to see it go shuddering on
down the stone mouth, the long gullet that runs

beneath factories, houses, trees new-fledged with green
and the lost graves of the city's innumerable dead.

The Gates

From terraced streets and tree-lined boulevards
they come with flowers to these high gates – so many,

passing beneath the porter's wintry gaze.
Their heads are bowed. They trudge up the wide path

but cast no shadow in the ashen light.
An ambulance drives through. Its darkened windows

mirror the clock-tower and the serried wards
to which it hastens with its unseen charge.

Flooded Air-Raid Shelter

The bolt slides back, the iron door creaks open –
mould-stink, damp, a scatter of tiny bones,

and the stairs descending into the flooded shaft.
His ghost-face wavers on that opaque glass.

Somewhere below, the dreadful chambers lie,
silent and cold, which cannot now be entered.

In the back-field a bonfire gusts and flares.
Smoke billows from the tall hospital chimney.

Escaped Prisoner

He stands on the high slate roof, his arms outspread,
and flings down at them angry inaudible words.

The morning sun strikes him, his red face shines –
a wingless angel on the brink of desperate flight.

What holds him back? The killing of a man,
the unbearable weight of a man's body broken.

Soon the black figures crawling along the ridge
will carry him off in chains for the doctor to cure.

The Carpenters

In their sunny workshop the carpenters are busy.
They measure, they cut; they cut, they do not look up,

they do not see the ward-windows open
or the patients in their grey-striped dressing-gowns

arranged in day-beds on the iron verandas.
They cut, they hammer. Dust drifts round their boots.

Shiny are the nails they hold in their thin lips.
Dark is the glue simmering in its pot.

The Laundry

In baskets to this place of polished tiles,
of copper and steel, these vats of scalding water,

these drums of air, the sheets and gowns are fetched
to be made clean. Again and yet again

the sick and dying soil them. The laundry-women
banter and laugh; their kindly faces glow.

The steam ascending into the girdered roof
is shot with sunlight and their silvery voices.

Autumn Night

The October sun withdraws, long shadows stretch
across the subtle hollows of the lawn:

dusk settling on the house – closed doors and windows,
the clatter of pans, the sound of water running.

In the tall Victorian wards the lamps are dimmed.
Out in the orchard, darkness feeds her children.

They sit in the uncut grass beneath the trees,
their hands in their laps, their eyes as pale as milk.

Porch Door, Evening

They step for a moment into the pool of light –
the doctor, the nurse, the sailor, the black-clad priest,

the engineer wiping his oily hands on a rag,
the quick, the dapper dancer, the keeper of horses,

and this one in Poor-Law grey with her lame leg
who goes limping off after the rest through the shadowy trees

singing. Listen: you can hear her still.
These, and so many more, briefly appearing.

High Sycamore

The wind at his back, he sways with the swaying tree:
late March, still leafless, the ash-grey bark gleaming.

He has climbed up into its delicate creel of branches
which creak as the air breathes among their bones –

distance, distance. Now high over the roofs he leans
and the muddy field, following with his gaze

an anonymous bird that bursts in a clatter of wings
from dripping bushes into the untrammelled air.

Some Trees, Some Creatures

March

The young man who has come to thin the birches
rides in his harness in the clean light he has made.
His orange helmet glows. The low March sun
ranges along the ridge – High Flatts, Birds Edge.

His shadow sways in ghastly silhouette
on the weather-blackened stone of the cottages.
You watch from the doorway, shadowless yourself.
The severed boughs tumble into the grass.

July

Arrow, needle, splinter of stellar light,
hawking above the reeds by the over-spill?
Steely flicker lost in the ripple-sheen:
"Look, there's another!" you cry. Dead in a week.

Or this in the dam itself, that can live for months,
with its vizored jaw hinged and fanged for prey?
Square Wood in leaf, its shifting veils of green
mirrored in quiet water at the dam-head.

November

Late and yet later. To the left of the steep track,
sycamore and oak aflame in the early dusk;
to the right, a stand of fir trees, gloomy crescent
trembling and hissing, though the cold air is still.

Where does the path come out? A scrawny fox
slips from the tall firs and lopes away
ahead of us down the hill. The cusp of winter,
clickering sticks turned incandescent with frost.

April

Not seeing me, you leave your hiding place
in the broken shade beneath the clump of birches.
The catkins quake and scatter their yellow dust,
and sunlight spills its coinage on the grass.

Our eyes meet for a moment. On the top road,
the rumble of wheels; a bird calling from the hedge.
Our eyes meet. For a moment I do not know
which one of us is alive, which one a ghost.

A Scattering of Ashes

for Jean Gregson 1921 – 2001

Out of the wicket gate and down the yard
to a sudden surf of barks where the farm dog
      leaps and pulls at his chain;
      on past the tyre-stack,

the five sky-blue drums weighted with rocks,
the derelict yawl, the slew of orange rope;
      at the shed's seaward end
      round into the wind,

this June day lithe and buxom that in winter
skelps off the bay and bends to its bleak will
      each stunted bush and tree;
      so, through the second gate –

the heavy iron frame drawn creaking back,
swung clangorously to – and out into the lane:
      hedge-banks of earth and stone,
      thorn-brake, campion, gorse,

small burrows running back into the dark:
the fall of unseen waters, murmur of speech –
      deaths and *marriages* – muffled
      in that green hush; at last

where the rutted track winds round a narrow cleft –
black rocks studded with thrift, the grey tide moiling –
      down over furrowed strata,
      across dykes of milk-white quartz,

into the tiny cove: an even light
on the sea's rumpled tin, on the idle stones
      that clink in its lift and fall,
      its salt ancestral breathing;

from the leeward cliff the solemn cry of choughs,
their nest high in a crack, and still the soft
       words falling, *children*, *grandchildren*:
       your ashes cast on the water;

then where the white rocks jut, a sleek brown head
emerging from the waves – two steady eyes
       whose wide incurious gaze
       the watchers on the shore

cannot sustain but, turning back too late,
see only the opal wake of its vanishing,
       the sky's vacant arch,
       the small waves at their feet …

Llŷn, Wales

How to Tell

for P.V.C.W.

1

In the darkness of pain
or pain's proleptic shadow
how to tell
from which bush
the small bird sings,
its call rising and falling –
if it is a bird and not
some human voice:
wind threading
through dry sticks
in haste to be elsewhere.

2

On the car radio
Beethoven's Seventh,
third movement,
miraculously rearranges
air and light,
cloud-shadow, trees,
the advancing road
and what we travel towards.
When it ends –
five abrupt chords –
everything is left
exactly as it was.

3

Tutelars of steel and light
arrayed at the bed-head,
flickering prognostications
in the dim sanctum,
oximeter, cannula, cardiograph,
sacs of clear liquid,
hiss of oxygen:
gowned and masked
your adepts come and go.
My hand on your muscular wounded arm,
you wait at the brink of your own myth,
your hand on mine, unrelinquishing.

Address Book

for A.E.W. 1915 – 2009

The address book is
down at the
bottom, buried

under last year's
holiday maps. It is
full except

for those strange letters
X and Z – mostly
in Father's

hand. Father,
you have been dead seven years.
Mother, your wife, has

crossed out
some, has added.
Her handwriting still

keeps your slope
though stiffer now, less
fluent. Thank you,

she says.
Now I can
get on.

1967

Tenure

Face to the pillow, drifting off to sleep,
you rehearse your familiar litany – this house,
your quilts, your kitchen-garden caught
in the sunlight of July – and one by one
trace back through a cloud of loves
your other houses: an August cornfield,
swallows hunting a line of oaks,
and the river's thin glare; then back and back
to the long garden of another place,
children silently at play
on the scorched lawn in the drought of '76
and a piano sounding through the French window;
and further still: an Edwardian flat,
the homes you lived in with your parents –
the dining-table you made your den,
a rough triangle of grass
and the amazing view far-off of your first home
from just across the street
where only a year or two before
a gun emplacement stood;
and then at last receding from yourself
to half-guessed things, to shadowy fragments
called up by the long-dead who wait
impossibly close at hand – cellar and terrace
and the grieving sigh of the forge;
till your breath slows and, step by step,
you are borne deeper still –
but into what place so dark and strange
that, risen to this new day,
for a moment you are lost for words?

VI

The Spacious Firmament on high,
With all the blue Etherial Sky ...

– Joseph Addison

Pilgrim

Propped on a bony elbow, head on hand,
and posed, so the guidebook says, "as you were found",
you stare from your glass case out into the dark
where we, still dazzled by the brilliant ache
of the fierce, Italian, midday, summer light
we thought to shelter from in this echoing vault,
stare back at you – that pinched and wizened face,
those shrivelled eyes, vacant and meaningless,
and the woollen habit, mouldering with age,
you wore when you came here on your pilgrimage
and by the closed confessional knelt down,
and slept, but did not wake, some rough homespun
that like your flesh stayed sweet and undecayed
a hundred years at least after you died.
Next morning when the sacristan unlocked,
and the first light streamed in, surely he balked
to see you lying as if sound asleep,
but when you would not stir, he took you up,
a stranger with no history and no name,
and laid your body in an empty tomb.

Who would have missed you when you didn't return?
Some wife or mother or son watching in vain
the steep washed-out path through the olive groves;
or, elsewhere, a stinking alleyway that curves
past squalid tenements down to a blind court.
A winter dusk, the stars already bright.
Two women murmuring in an upper room.
Somewhere, a dog barks. Wood-smoke. A crackle of flame
leaping into the bitter air. He must
have sketched out something of the sort, have glossed
for himself the singular mystery of your end
in this mansion built to house God's vagabond
and serious Word – whose simple colours spread
on valley and hill, on orchard, field and wood

their narrative of suffering and reward
and rendered them iconic. Beast and bird,
tares in the counted crop, hail, wind and rain,
each had its proper place in the design.

But whatever you came here for or left behind,
the story made you its creature in the end.
Next day he found the heavy stone pushed back
that sealed your tomb; and you, as if to rebuke
his huddling you away in that strict cell,
rested once more beside the confessional
in stubborn sleep. Startled, what did he think?
(What do we think?) That some brave boys for a prank
had come at dead of night and delivered you
from your grim lodging? And what was he to do
but shut you away again in that cold lair?
But the third day you had escaped once more
and once more waited for the priest as if
still dreaming of absolution in this life.
This time he did not put you back but placed
your mutinous body in a wooden chest
in the sacristy. You did not stir again.
Withering away at last to a dark sign,
you lingered here for your viaticum,
so long delayed, and the long-imagined doom.
Now haloed with damp, your Saints and Virgins spoil,
their figured histories barely legible
on the crazed plaster, while the Cherubim
who, keeping watch above you, spangled the gloom
with accurate blue and gold, fade from our eyes
in a feathered cloud of fugitive pinks and greys.

What more in this for us, who step aside
and, catching each other's gaze as if to avoid
your arid, empty stare, know there's no art
can resurrect a life, its fluent weight,
its miraculous scape and scope? Like a twist of fire
we track a moment through the dark to flare,
howling or sighing, into silence. Fixed

by the old tale, by the guidebook's jaunty text,
your journey stalled forever in this hush.
Yet something survived – stark image of our flesh,
emblem of constancy, embodied faith –
the soft, unchronicled lapse of your warm breath.
Corporeal still, still not quite fallen to dust,
even now you must bear witness to your Christ.

Behind us a door creaks open, shuts. A stir
of shadows. Sandals click on the tiled floor.
The priest goes whispering by in his black soutane.
He nods at us but already he has gone –
as soon we too must leave this ancient house,
its smell of incense, its glass sarcophagus.
And so we step once more into the light
that fills the little square, where we shall sit
in the shade of green umbrellas for an hour
sipping at something long and cold and clear.

The bright day slows. The gaudy banners droop
in the still air, and the town dogs are asleep.
Unruffled water shines at the basin's brim.
Aura and shimmer and gleam: a lambent calm
lies on each visible thing – on the far hills
that we must cross before night, the ochre walls,
cypress and olive and vine. As if inlaid
on the sky's lapis dome, so high it could
be motionless, a glittering silver plane
describes in ice and fire its urgent line.

Montefalco

Labourers in the Vineyard

Where grey woods climb a steep gorge
and spread out from its rocky verge
to occupy with oak and thorn
a long-abandoned house and barn,
three men have toiled through the hot day
clearing the vines – a husbandry
these two young women in their jeep
have driven with register and map
up the white road from town to check.
Sullenly they watch them park
their four-track in the dusty shade.
One has thrown his hook aside
and scans a buzzard in the sky;
his fellow shrugs and walks away;
the third stands fast upon the ground
their labour in the vineyard earned.
(Look! By his foot a lizard hides …)
They spread their map and point. He nods.
Among the bushes by the track
a fourth man lurks. In the blue dark,
surely thinking himself unseen,
he drops his britches and squats down.

Boccabuto

The Wolf of Gubbio

When the great Wolf of Gubbio made his pact
with the fabled Saint – to quit, for gifts of food,
scraps left in doorways or tossed down a damp yard,
his predatory habit, who had stalked
through grove and garden at will, taking, unchecked,
stray lambs and goats and in his furious pride
making grown men afraid to walk abroad –
what did his fellows think of the trick he had worked?

That, hunter turned scavenger, he had betrayed his kind,
had sinned against nature, an outcast to be shunned?
Or did they envy him his harmless ease?
The Saint taught the power of love; the Wolf obeyed.
The small birds listened warily from the boughs.
Across the waste the silvery shadows sped.

Gubbio

Goshawk

So dense the ancient wood,
    so choked by stubborn thorn
    at the edge of the steep road,
that he stands, almost unseen,
    in sunlight, as if perhaps
    fearing to go on
into that green eclipse,
    that canopy of gloom.
    Half a dozen steps,
and leaves encompass him.
    Blades of beaten foil
    quiver with a faint gleam,
and the gilded berries reel
    and tinkle in the brake.
    Let him press deeper still
down aisles of elm and oak
    through tangled undergrowth
    into the lustrous dark,
till, far from any path,
    earth swales into a fen,
    its rank mephitic breath
drifting blue and green
    above a Stygian mire;
    and there such noises din
into his wondering ear –
    the howl and yelp and hiss
    of anguish and despair
risen from that black fosse –
    that he is brought to a stand,
    hollow and comfortless,
and from that desolate bound
    sees by the errant flames
    that, glimmering, coil and wind

above those shattered limbs,
    those trunks, those gaping heads,
    the scandalous martyrdoms.
But now the colonnades
    of stiff high-raftered oaks
    stir as the wind floods
spilling a peal of barks,
    a bold commanding shout;
    and the dream-vision breaks,
dissolving on that note
    in pattering leaves, in sun,
    in the river's agile fret
round rocks as white as bone.
    And he will turn aside
    and follow the waters down
to where the narrow road
    cuts its bright curve
    through scrub and flourishing weed.
There in an olive grove,
    two men wait by the track.
    Perched on his falconer's glove
the younger carries a hawk –
    white eyebrow, orange eye,
    the beak's trim brown hook.
His fellow, dropped to one knee,
    fondles a brace of hounds,
    brindled and iron-grey.
Beyond them the valley winds
    under the broad spur
    where the little hill-town stands,
sun-struck and austere.
    The towers are jasper and gold.
    The brave pennons flare.
The hawk quarters the field.

Pieve San Nicolò, Assisi

Assisi

after a sonnet by Gabriele D'Annunzio

Peace? Of a kind – in which is bodied forth
    the torrent thrashing down its scour
in passionate frays and ravellings of white foam;
    and blue-grey cypresses aspire
towards the sun like wrathful ghosts of flame
        from the hard earth.

Peace of a kind – dusk and the barren stones.
    In the cool breath of evening prayer,
the impetuous spills and slippages run pale,
    and the Saint's flesh, kindled by desire
to escape the flesh, falls bleeding upon a snarl
        of rose-thorns.

Madonna and Child

Not pollen of lily or rose or the fine scales
flicked from a butterfly wing, but stone-dust, wood-
dust, ash, adrift in the steep sun that falls
around her from high windows, azure, gold,
earth-red, the shimmer of incarnation – who kneels,
and crosses herself, and prays, her dark eyes turned
to meet the light: its graceful skeins and swirls
dazzle her for a moment and leave her blind.

The faithful come and go. Cradling their son,
her husband waits till she returns to him –
quite at his ease, for this has happened before.
Beside the altar, the tall candles burn.
His eyes reflect their shafts of aureate flame,
which flutter a little in the unsteady air.

Santa Maria Assunta, Spoleto

Paragliders

What folk are these who have come,
by car, on foot, up the track to this high place,
    gathering after their long climb
in twos and threes upon that shelf of grass?
    Look how the August sun
that gilds the scattered stones and the green blades
    with ordinary light has drawn
a fleeting glory round their quiet heads.

Before their feet, the earth
falls sheer. From such a height the sunlit plain,
    the little town, its intricate wreath
of roads, factory and farm and wood, all turn
    to intricate chequer-work:
patches of gold and umber stretch away
    southward to far hills that break
in dove-grey strokes of cloud against the sky.

Above, a rush of wings,
a stirring as of linen ruched and quilled
    or a fiery exaltation of tongues –
as if, swept up from that narrow stony field
    on the cool tide of the air
and borne aloft above the grassy summit
    unwearying in arc and spire,
our earthly freight at last might prove pure spirit.

But now another, a girl,
sets down her heavy burden on the turf
    and, kneeling, rigs the blue sail
that soon will bear her out into the gulf.
    Already the quickening wind
has breathed into its cells and caught her weight,
    and she, close-lipped as though she scorned
to tread upon the earth, leaps up to meet

       its hurrying blind embrace.
The watchers tilt their heads, a young man points,
    and out into the bright abyss,
as if air and fire were her true elements,
       she is drawn up. The sun
flares on the ribbed arch of her wing, on the flock
    of wings that – turn and counter-turn –
beneath the vault of heaven shift and tack,

       till, slanting aside, she sweeps
from the zenith out over gully and cliff through the lofts
    of summer air and, moth-like, drops
softly down; and the scurrying wind lifts,
       and the trees shake out their skirts,
and earth flows up to catch her where she falls
    among hens and scampering children and goats,
and the dusty farm-dog yaps at her flickering heels.

Monte Subasio, Assisi: 15th August, 2002

VII

The Rainbow

I am but a ghost of the shore.

– Maggi Hambling

... oracular
Notations of the wild, the ruinous waste ...

– Wallace Stevens

1

What end is there for all this watery noise,
tumult of wind and wave, the breakers' heave
and dull collapsing roar?

As far as the eye can see, wild delugings
of grey and green and black, scrolls of white foam
jumbled and purposeless, the flurry and skirr of spray.

In all that dismal waste no sign of land,
no bird scouring the crests,
no fraught vessel wallowing and yawing.

Only a chaos of unceasing change made new
beneath the form and accident of paint
into unchangingness – spatter and swirl,

the bodily trace of brush and hand and arm:
"Sunrise, December 2008". A smear of red
streams like a fiery pennant in the east.

2

When James, Archbishop Ussher of Armagh,
heir to St Patrick, died in 1656,
learning and piety having cured, it seems,

his one great defect, loyalty to the crown,
Cromwell, the Lord Protector,
sanctioned his interment in the Abbey.

Yet of his learning – Hebrew, Latin, Greek –
only the chronology survived,
printed in almanacs and Bibles

for two and a half centuries after his death.
On every page, for instance, of Dr Eadie's
National Illustrated Family Bible of 1851:

leather on boards, metal clasps and edges,
the dates given a second time
in a handy index at the back.

Thus in the year 4004 BC,
as Ussher from inerrant Holy Writ
scrupulously calculated – in modern terms,

the evening of a Saturday in October –
God made the world, gathering together
into one place the waters under heaven

that dry land might appear.
And here are the generations of Adam,
and here the Flood

when all the fountains of the deep were broken up
and heaven's windows opened. Terror and panic,
the risen waters engulfing crops and houses,

drowning all but those a thrawn creator
selected for the unwieldy ark.
To the good archbishop this was no mere fable

betokening God's ordinance and prevision,
but actual as his own life:
exile in England, capture by Welsh brigands,

his death reported, his epitaph prepared;
or watching from a house in St Martin's Lane
the execution of the Lord's Anointed.

He passed out when the men in black vizards
put up the monarch's hair.
Would Lyell's geology have made him blench?

By 1851 the Reverend Eadie
had science argue his own case,
the very mountains offering "uniform proof"

that once upon a time "the sea
spread over the highest summits,
shells and skeletons of fish &c

having been found there". Imagine Ussher's ghost
pacing the Thames-side streets,
rehearsing still his perfect reckoning, estranged

from a universe grown infinite and schismatic.
The river pours away, taking into itself
the outflow of the city's forgotten drains,

sliding down past Greenwich and Gravesend,
mist on the Essex marshes, gulls yammering at sunset,
Sheerness, Foulness, and so to the North Sea,

which swells and surges fathoms-deep where once
over low hills reindeer and aurochs ran
and flocks of wildfowl wintered in tidal pools.

3

Tell the old tale backwards. How long passed
since they were spared their wicked neighbours' fate
and changed by the gods into two trees – an oak, a lime –

that neither might be left to grieve for the other,
reward for sheltering under their humble roof
great Jove and his companion, Mercury?

Tell the old tale backwards.
Let the rough bark grow soft, the roots draw in,
and the stiff branches turn once more into arms.

Let the eye open, the tongue be freed in the mouth's cleft
that laughter may fall lightly into the air –
as their ancient, paired, separate, human selves

step forth and, looking down, behold
the flood abate, the lake dwindle to a pond,
and the marsh, swallowing itself away,

bottom into solid ground.
There as before their small cottage stands
and, beyond, their drowned neighbours' houses –

chimneys purling smoke in the still air,
closed doors, walled gardens,
the certainties of containment –

as if those pitiless waters had not been;
and church and school appear,
phone-box and petrol-station,

and all the loved and sinful world they knew,
towards which hand in hand they walk,
entering again the history of their lives.

4

Where was he standing, what was his point
of vantage when the photograph was taken –
black and white, barely two inches wide

and dated on the back in smudged pencil June 1950?
A park lake fixed in sunlight, a line of trees;
out on the water a single rowing boat,

a man seated in the stern, a boy at the oars,
the shining instant caught
by his long-lost pre-war Leica.

Or this? A memory, undated:
the lake drained, low early-evening sun
raking the trees – alder or willow or oak –

mud that had reeked for days now dry and cracked,
and there a row of wooden piles
that might have been a jetty once, dead leaves,

a dead swan, its neck hooked back,
the breeze ruffling its plumage, but also
an iron bedstead, the carcass of a pram,

a set of railings, their green points still sharp.
Random depositions made by whom?
Photo, memory: what distances between?

*

And this? A causeway eight yards wide,
some sixty thousand posts in five rows
stretching a mile along the fenland edge.

Open water to the north, the timber platform
guarded against that bleak and deadly quarter
by an outer palisade of angled stakes.

To the south, embayed by higher ground,
good summer grazing for the beasts –
paddocks and drove-ways hedged with quickthorn.

And placed in the shallows on the southern side
hundreds of votive gifts,
which lay unseen for two millennia

till archaeology returned them to the light:
spearheads deliberately bent,
a bronze sword, the blade doubled at a flaw,

pins snapped in half, broken bracelets of shale,
and scores of white pebbles. To what end
these small obscure devotions

continuing long after the fen flooded
and the folk moved west to drier ground?
Imperfect resurrection, strange apocalypse,

stripped of their histories, they shrink
from signs to evidence: a winter day,
sleet volleying in the wind, the reeds shaking.

Across the open mere a fitful sun
breaks in glints and signatures of itself,
flint-black, illegible and brief.

*

Centuries before the Romans built their shrine
in the wooded combe above the river
the cold spring came tinkling out of the hill.

Now it spills down its channel into the pool.
Moss on the stone, the glint of coins at the bottom –
thank-offering, petition to what imagined gods?

Safe in the trees' swaying ark
the dove calls her morning call,
roo-coo, roo-coo,

and there by the barrier you stand –
in the photograph, in memory –
an audio-guide at your ear,

nymph of these clear waters, water-nymph,
smiling as even now you do
in sunlight somewhere near at hand.

5

Unseen and silent, I wear a shifting cloak
of iridescent blue, of grey, of white,
and keep for weeks and months my head well down,

fed on the violent energies of division.
Leviathan thinks to equal me in his dark world,
but I am myself a world and contain worlds.

Worlds I destroy. Fire bursts forth from me.
With terrible precision
I lay waste to cities, to entire nations,

imposing everywhere my covenanted will.
I brook no defence.
My imperium circles the earth.

Yet I, too, am under strict command.
A cryptic word directs from some far-off place
my watery passages, my rise and fall. What am I?

6

for Irene, i.m. Nel Drieduite-de Heide (1941 – 2007)

Zwabber, her English sheepdog, heard it first
and ran cowering into the lakeside grass:
a whirring, a low humming,

that might have been inside her head
but was not; then under monitory clouds
a strange ball of light

that travelled above the water and, seconds after,
struck a block of flats and killed a child.
Fearful, she crouched beside her dog,

but what she heard and what she saw was this:
the heavy drone of planes over Rotterdam,
she and her sisters hurrying through the streets,

a soldier, stick in hand, shouting in German
(angry or urging them to safety?),
flame and smoke and dust;

then the polders flooded, the hunger-winter,
which miraculously she survived.
All this from one of her long handwritten letters,

a correspondence lasting almost a lifetime,
which began with a mistake,
a misconstruction both of you would laugh at.

February 1st, 1953,
the full moon two days gone.
A deep depression south of Iceland

sweeps howling into the North Sea,
hurricane winds driving a spring tide
down through that starless funnel.

At 2 a.m. the first dykes are topped,
and the storm-surge bursts in across the fields.
By families they drown, and all their beasts,

house and barn and church carried away,
shattered timber floating in the streets
and the many dead.

At the Groenendijk the mayor commandeers
a barge, *De Twee Gebroeders*,
and has her captain steer her into the breach.

She turns in the thundering waters like a gate
and locks against the dyke.
Two provinces are saved.

But you, a child of eight in Liverpool,
knew little of this, picturing instead
a neat Dutch house like those in your story book

with a little Dutch girl perched alone on the roof,
the brown water lapping at the walls,
and wrote your own first letter,

while she in truth lived safe at home
in a first-floor apartment with her parents.
And so it began, the shared chronicle

you patched and pieced between you
year after year in a bright quilt;
and not a single letter went astray.

The dykes were mended. Barrier and sluice
shelter the Zeeland estuaries –
silt, mud-flat, dune –

and manage the tidal flow of three great rivers
through vast lagoons of salt or brackish water,
though still the sea rises, the land sinks.

7

High water. Over the drowned villages the tide
idles and lolls, their fabled bells unheard.
Flocks of brant-geese call from the flooded marsh,

*off on their long ancestral flight to the north.
The early rain has turned to a fine smirr
which the sun will sign with its illusive bow.*

VIII

Non c'è pensiero che imprigioni il fulmine
ma chi ha veduto la luce non se ne priva.

– Eugenio Montale

Nuit Blanche

You turn the key and enter. The room is white –
white walls, white floor, white ceiling, curtains, bed –
everything emptied of colour as if colour –
even the lily's drained passionate white,
apple-blossom, orange-blossom, pear – might burn and burn,
nothing to save the maddened flesh from itself.

Bone-white, ash-white: snow's feathered silence
drifting into the dark; and we must breathe
as slow as those ghost-flakes; and soft and slow
your stirring at first light, the awakened blood
glowing – that deep bloom – in cheek and lip.

Apple

after the Spanish of Lope de Vega

When I went riding out
the sun was behind the hill.
She leaned from her balcony,
from the iron balustrade,
and tossed an apple down.
Its flesh was crisp and white.
Had I tossed one up to her,
I swear it would have turned
    to blossom again.

When I went riding out
the sun was behind the hill.
Her grey eyes shone
in the moon's cold light.
What did she know of love?
She thought it just a game.
Had I tossed her an apple,
I swear it would have turned
    to blossom again.

The sun was behind the hill
when she leaned from her balcony
and tossed an apple down,
the moon in her grey eyes
glittering like ice.
Had I tossed one up to her,
I swear it would have turned –
petals of sharp snow –
    to blossom again.

A Pretty Position

If knowing when to stop
is the mark of a true artist,

how much might be learned
from an hour's blind

obedience cunningly required,
in which we could lay down

the choices that consume us
and melt into a tutelage of small cries,

each an inkling of subtler nakednesses,
more instructive crafts yet to come.

In the absence of contexts,
categories no longer exist.

Tell me, then, what insinuating art
produced, one by one,

those elegant grapes,
those sassy cherries flushed

with invisible sweetness?
Tyranny is a very pretty position.

A connoisseur of such things,
how can you bear

the Midas touch
of so much possibility?

At Middelburg

Alas, the miniature town was closed:
through chained railings,

beyond wintry flowerbeds,
not even a glimpse

of the antique houses
scaled to knee-height,

crannied rooms
in which, though tired,

we could so easily have imagined
Lilliputian rituals

of sex and birth and death
and fashioned for ourselves

with a sweet hauteur
wary fictions of the real.

Ornithology at Sumburgh Head

Sea-light riffles the leaves of our field-guide.
Scaup, phalarope ... Not that, not that.

Your lips pucker in a moue of annoyance,
and the wind grows stronger.

But this is not the moonlit pond
where once I skimmed flat stones,

each skip and jook a diminishing white letter
rippling to silence in the glassy dark;

nor yet that pool at the glen-head
in which I plunged one summer's day,

gasping for breath in its sudden cold embrace,
and put all self-respecting birds to flight.

(Now tell me whose idea *that* was.)
Your airy laughter echoed from the rocks.

Scaup, phalarope ...
Fulmar, kittiwake, shag ...

Not this, not that.
By the waters' green lapse,

by their abounding roar,
the shimmering vertigo of distance.

Trumpets and Castanets

Despite my protest, the CD repeats
endlessly your favourite track:

trumpets and castanets,
fierce and tender – like your dance,

your voice as you sing
without meaning, without

distinguishable words.
You are fragrant with lust,

but there are other stairs to climb,
a void replete with stifled cries.

A curriculum laid down elsewhere
defines what we are, a power

like God's or the state's
that passes understanding and makes

all of us transparent,
known through and through.

Steel teeth engage, traps clatter open,
close again, belts turn and slip,

darkness hinging on itself
somewhere out of sight.

Better surely to move, a masquerade
of light and air, unrecognized

through the world's passages.
Your blue-grey eyes glitter.

Smiling, you take my hand,
and now the music starts again

its blessed maddening rote.
A foreignness begins.

On the Coast of Phaeacia

Grizzled and naked,
the half-drowned sailor

drew himself up from those salt lips,
from that whetted nick,

crept under a bush,
dreaming of kelp, of white arms.

Come dripping from the sea,
what strong cords bind him,

that he must lie, unbidden guest,
anchored thus in himself?

Insignia

To give up pretensions is as much a blessing
as to have them gratified:

the act should be its own reward,
the knack of purposeful attention

that arms us against the dread of not existing.
It is for this reason, you say,

we must lay titles aside, insignia of rank,
the repertoire of prophylactic ornament.

Establish, therefore, a clean point of origin,
each new position thereafter

an evolution not to be denied.
But the anguished lust to return,

to make present the histories we have lived,
turns into fiction whatever it lights on.

Let these, then, be proxy:
at your throat a choker of black beads,

your ear-lobes weighted by these ebony drops'
all but weightless weight.

The Visit

after a fragmentary Greek epitaph

Your ancient car parked on the dusty lane,
soon you'll come walking through the summer heat
    up a field of burnished grass
  which, opening for your sandaled feet,
      will let them pass,
then brush together at your heels again.

By the stone wall you will stand shading your eyes.
A weft of brightness hangs in the still air,
    and the valley falls away
  to a peacock sea all shimmer and glare
      in its wide bay,
above which, fast and low, a brown bird flies.

A moment, and you climb on through the trees
and lose yourself in shade. But no dark place
    can hold you long: the light
  that prints its shadows on your face
      will lead you out
among white lilies loud with golden bees.

And you will bring a gift – of wine, or bread,
some green herbs from the garden – which we shall share,
    twining a bright wreath
  of talk in the dry unmoving air
      that settles beneath
the cypresses. Things said, things left unsaid.

The unhastening sun will steal into the west,
and on the tranquil roof white doves will croon
    their soft adagio
  that solemnly all afternoon
      pace to and fro,
heedless of us in their amorous unrest.

The Cyclist

Behind the beach-huts' weathered pinks and greens
low dunes run inland – sea holly, marram and spurge;
a blue flag stiffens in the breeze. The small verandas
look out over banks of rose-grey shingle and sand,
and drifts of seaweed tangled like dark hair,
towards upturned boats, and long groynes, and the bay.
In the foreground, on a path that soon leads off

outside the frame, someone pedals a bike.
A man or a woman? Hard to tell at that angle.
Its wheels are a silvery blur. In the dim huts
the salty air hangs still. The sea that folds
in its endless glittering lapse those tiny grains
shelves into deeper waters, while out in the offing
soft tongues of light flicker across the sky.

For a moment you catch me up, and hand in hand
we enter the next gallery. What shall it be?
A double portrait, faded and speckled with age?
A neat stone bridge spanning a waterfall?
A night-piece? Or this – three peonies set in a glass,
their wine-red ruffles chrismed with beads of light?
And still the cyclist has not passed from view.

Notes

Cover Image: Paul Klee, *Gestirne über bösen Häusern* [*Stars above evil houses*], 1916, 79, watercolour on primed linen on cardboard, 19/20 x 21.2/22.2 cm, Merzbacher Kunststiftung.

Section I: Epigraph: John Bunyan, *The Pilgrim's Progress*.

"The Escape": after an etching by John A McPake R.E., "Noah's Ka" (1981) in the collection of the poet.

"The House": Epigraph: from *Galgenlieder* [Gallows Songs], 1905.

"The President Flies Home": Italicized lines are adapted from the Vanity Fair episode in John Bunyan's *The Pilgrim's Progress*.

"The Angel": Epigraph: "Wenhaston" is pronounced WENerstun.

"The Angel 2": Eunice Bagster illustrated editions of *The Pilgrim's Progress* published, from 1845, by her father, Samuel Bagster. Foxe: i.e. John Foxe's *Book of Martyrs* (1583).

"The Angel 4": Santa Maria del Fiore: the Duomo, Florence.

"The Angel 5": This section refers to the massacre at Jedwabne, Eastern Poland, on 10th July 1941, responsibility for which has been the subject of much controversy.

"The Angel 6": HMS *Sirius* was named for the Dog Star. The ship in which Paul sailed on from Malta to Rome was *The Two Brothers*, named for the brothers Castor and Pollux, tutelary gods of mariners. Cf. "The Rainbow 6".

"The Angel 7": cf. Revelation 8.

Section III: Epigraph: from *Playing the Human Game: The Collected Poems of Alfred Brendel* trans. Richard Stokes (London: Phaidon Press, 2010).

"Clown Face, Ronald Reagan, Stocking Head": Charlie Cairoli (1910-1980) was a celebrated white-face clown.

"Small Scenes from a Life": Epigraph: "I have kept myself light so the ferry-boat will sink less" from "On Voit", in *Pensées sous les nuages* (Paris: Editions Gallimard, 1983) – Jaccottet alludes to the scene in *Aeneid* VI in which Charon's barge groans under the living weight of Aeneas.

Section V: Epigraph: G. B. Shaw, *Heartbreak House* (1919).

"Jane, Aged Twenty, Takes Tea at the Big House": The rhymes are derived from Shakespeare's Sonnet 20.

"Black Kites, Salty, Jesus Bird": The Dry is the dry season in Australia. A salty is a salt-water crocodile. The Jesus bird is so called because, stepping on partly submerged lily pads, it appears to walk on water.

"The Hospital": The sequence is set in a large hospital in Liverpool. It had opened in 1864 as a workhouse; when the Poor Law system ended in the 1930s, it held some 2,500 inmates. The hospital's extensive grounds were bisected by a deep railway cutting. Walton Jail is less than a mile from the hospital. Prisoners were sometimes brought in for treatment. By the 1950s, a small number of elderly men and women, admitted under the Poor Law, still lived semi-independently in special accommodation. Their distinctive clothing was cut from grey cloth.

"Some Trees, Some Creatures": In Yorkshire, a dam is a body of water enclosed by a dam. Dragonflies spend part of their life-cycle in water as *nymphs*, which are ferocious predators.

Section VI: Epigraph: Joseph Addison, "Ode" (*The Spectator*, 23rd August, 1712).

"Pilgrim": The poem tells the story associated with the mummy of an anonymous pilgrim from the Middle Ages displayed in Sant'Agostino, Montefalco, Umbria, and known as "Il Beato Pellegrino".

"Paragliders": On 15th August occurs the Feast of the Assumption of the Virgin Mary. Mount Subasio, above Assisi, rises to 1290 metres and gives stunning views across the Umbrian plain.

"The Rainbow": Epigraphs: Maggi Hambling, *The Sea* (Salford Quays: Lowry Press, 2009); Wallace Stevens, "The Doctor of Geneva" (*Harmonium*, 1923).

"The Rainbow 1": This section refers to a painting by Maggi Hambling C.B.E. (collection of the poet).

"The Rainbow 2": The final tercet refers to the mesolithic landscape concealed beneath the North Sea. Until c.8000 BC Britain was part of mainland Europe; the Channel did not exist.

"The Rainbow 3": cf. the story of Baucis and Philemon, Ovid, *Metamorphoses*, 8.612.

"The Rainbow 4": The second part concerns Flag Fen, a bronze-age site near Peterborough, Cambridgeshire. The third part is set at Chedworth Roman villa in Gloucestershire.

"The Rainbow 5": A submarine armed with nuclear warheads.

"The Rainbow 6": The disastrous storm-surge and consequent floods of 1st February 1953 caused severe damage and loss of life on both sides of the North Sea, particularly in East Anglia and the southern Netherlands.

"The Rainbow 6": "*De Twee Gebroeders*": The Two Brothers – cf. "The Angel 6".

"The Rainbow 7": "the drowned villages" – such as Dunwich, Suffolk. In the middle ages Dunwich was a sizeable town, much of which was lost to the North Sea in the thirteenth century. The sea's depredations continue to this day. Dunwich lies four miles along the coast from Southwold, where the Suffolk-born artist Maggi Hambling has her studio (cf. Section 1). According to legend, migrating geese were the souls of the dead flying to their eternal home.

Section VIII: Epigraph: "No thought can imprison the lightning, | but he who once has seen its light cannot live without it." – from "Per album" in *La bufera e altro* (Milan, 1957).

Acknowledgements

I am grateful to fellow poets Chris Preddle and Susan de Sola for their editorial insights and to my publisher, Philip Hoy, for his patience and encouragement over many years.

My thanks, too, to the editors of the journals in which the following poems appeared, sometimes in earlier versions:

The Alabama Literary Review: "The Stones", "Manifesto", "Five Wasps", "Address Book", "Nuit Blanche" and "A Pretty Position".

New Walk: "The Angel".

The Dark Horse: "Pilgrim" (under the title "Il Beato Pellegrino").

The Hudson Review: "Goshawk" and "Paragliders".

"Jane, Aged Twenty, Takes Tea at the Big House" was published in *Fashioned Pleasures: Twenty-Four Poets Play Bouts-Rimés with a Shakespearean Sonnet* (University of Wisconsin-Madison: Parallel Press, 2005).

"The House" and "Insignia" were included in *Versions of the North: Contemporary Yorkshire Poetry*, edited by Ian Parks (Nottingham: Five Leaves Publications, 2013).

Finally, I should like to thank Mr. and Mrs. Werner Merzbacher of Zürich for permission to reproduce Paul Klee's painting *Gestirne über bösen Häusern* on the front cover.

Your white teeth strip from the willow rod
its green bark: bees hum in the wall.

A Note about the Author

Clive Watkins is a poet, translator, critic and editor. He was born in Sheffield, U.K., in 1945. His verse has appeared widely in the U.K. and the U.S.A. and was represented in the anthology *Versions of the North: Contemporary Yorkshire Poetry* (2013). His first collection, *Jigsaw*, was published by Waywiser in 2003. His long poem *Little Blue Man* was published as a chapbook by Sea Biscuit Press in 2013. He has read at venues in the U.K. – amongst others, at Grasmere (for the Wordsworth Trust) and at Oxford University – and in the U.S.A. and Greece. He has written essays for various journals on subjects as diverse as Conrad Aiken, Wallace Stevens, Eugenio Montale, Edward Thomas, E. J. Scovell and Michael Longley. At his retirement he was the head teacher of a prominent high school whose origins go back to the Middle Ages. He lives in Yorkshire, England.

Other Books from Waywiser

POETRY
Al Alvarez, *New & Selected Poems*
Chris Andrews, *Lime Green Chair*
George Bradley, *A Few of Her Secrets*
Geoffrey Brock, *Voices Bright Flags*
Robert Conquest, *Blokelore & Blokesongs*
Robert Conquest, *Penultimata*
Morri Creech, *Field Knowledge*
Morri Creech, *The Sleep of Reason*
Peter Dale, *One Another*
Erica Dawson, *Big-Eyed Afraid*
B. H. Fairchild, *The Art of the Lathe*
David Ferry, *On This Side of the River: Selected Poems*
Jeffrey Harrison, *The Names of Things: New & Selected Poems*
Joseph Harrison, *Identity Theft*
Joseph Harrison, *Someone Else's Name*
Joseph Harrison, ed., *The Hecht Prize Anthology, 2005-2009*
Anthony Hecht, *Collected Later Poems*
Anthony Hecht, *The Darkness and the Light*
Carrie Jerrell, *After the Revival*
Stephen Kampa, *Bachelor Pad*
Rose Kelleher, *Bundle o' Tinder*
Mark Kraushaar, *The Uncertainty Principle*
Matthew Ladd, *The Book of Emblems*
Dora Malech, *Shore Ordered Ocean*
Eric McHenry, *Potscrubber Lullabies*
Eric McHenry and Nicholas Garland, *Mommy Daddy Evan Sage*
Timothy Murphy, *Very Far North*
Ian Parks, *Shell Island*
V. Penelope Pelizzon, *Whose Flesh is Flame, Whose Bone is Time*
Chris Preddle, *Cattle Console Him*
Shelley Puhak, *Guinevere in Baltimore*
Christopher Ricks, ed., *Joining Music with Reason:*
34 Poets, British and American, Oxford 2004-2009
Daniel Rifenburgh, *Advent*
W. D. Snodgrass, *Not for Specialists: New & Selected Poems*
Mark Strand, *Almost Invisible*
Mark Strand, *Blizzard of One*
Bradford Gray Telford, *Perfect Hurt*
Matthew Thorburn, *This Time Tomorrow*
Cody Walker, *Shuffle and Breakdown*
Deborah Warren, *The Size of Happiness*
Clive Watkins, *Jigsaw*

Other Books from Waywiser

Richard Wilbur, *Anterooms*
Richard Wilbur, *Mayflies*
Richard Wilbur, *Collected Poems 1943-2004*
Norman Williams, *One Unblinking Eye*
Greg Williamson, *A Most Marvelous Piece of Luck*

FICTION
Gregory Heath, *The Entire Animal*
Mary Elizabeth Pope, *Divining Venus*
K. M. Ross, *The Blinding Walk*
Gabriel Roth, *The Unknowns**
Matthew Yorke, *Chancing It*

ILLUSTRATED
Nicholas Garland, *I wish …*
Eric McHenry and Nicholas Garland, *Mommy Daddy Evan Sage*

NON-FICTION
Neil Berry, *Articles of Faith: The Story of British Intellectual Journalism*
Mark Ford, *A Driftwood Altar: Essays and Reviews*
Richard Wollheim, *Germs: A Memoir of Childhood*

*Co-published with Picador